OUTDOOR ADVENTURE

FRESHWATER FISHING

BY GEORGE PENDERGAST

Gareth Stevens PUBLISHING

HOT TOPICS

Please visit our website, www.garethstevens.com. For a free color catalog of all our high-quality books, call toll free 1-800-542-2595 or fax 1-877-542-2596.

Pendergast, George.
Freshwater fishing / by George Pendergast.
p. cm. — (Outdoor adventure)
Includes index.
ISBN 978-1-4824-1231-4 (pbk.)
ISBN 978-1-4824-1237-6 (6-pack)
ISBN 978-1-4824-1493-6 (library binding)
1. Fishing — Juvenile literature. I. Title.
SH445.P46 2015
799.1—d23

First Edition

Published in 2015 by
Gareth Stevens Publishing
111 East 14th Street, Suite 349
New York, NY 10003

Designer: Nick Domiano
Editor: Ryan Nagelhout

Photo credits: Cover, p. 1 Wally Eberhart/Visuals Unlimited/Getty Images; cover texture Yuriy Boyko /Shutterstock.com; cover ribbon blinkblink/Shutterstock.com; pp. 4-5 Darrin Klimek/Thinkstock.com; pp. 6-7 Maria Teijeiro/Thinkstock.com; pp. 8-9 Paul Souders/Photodisc/Thinkstock.com; pp. 10-11 dcwcreations/Shutterstock.com; pp. 12-13 Pinosub/Shutterstock.com; pp. 14-15 OlegDoroshin/Shutterstock.com; pp. 16-17 liveslow/iStock/Thinkstock.com; p. 19 © iStockphoto.com/Drbouz; pp. 20-21 Deklofenak/Shutterstock.com; p. 23 Vsevolodizotov/Shutterstock.com; pp. 24-25 Stanislav Komogorov/Shutterstock.com; pp. 26-27 Photo Africa/ Shutterstock.com; pp. 28-29 © iStockphoto.com/Rezus; p. 30 (lure) Sters/ Shutterstock.com; p. 30 (life jacket) objectsforall/Shutterstock.com.

Printed in the United States of America

CPSIA compliance information: Batch #CS15GS: For further information contact Gareth Stevens, New York, New York at 1-800-542-2595.

CONTENTS

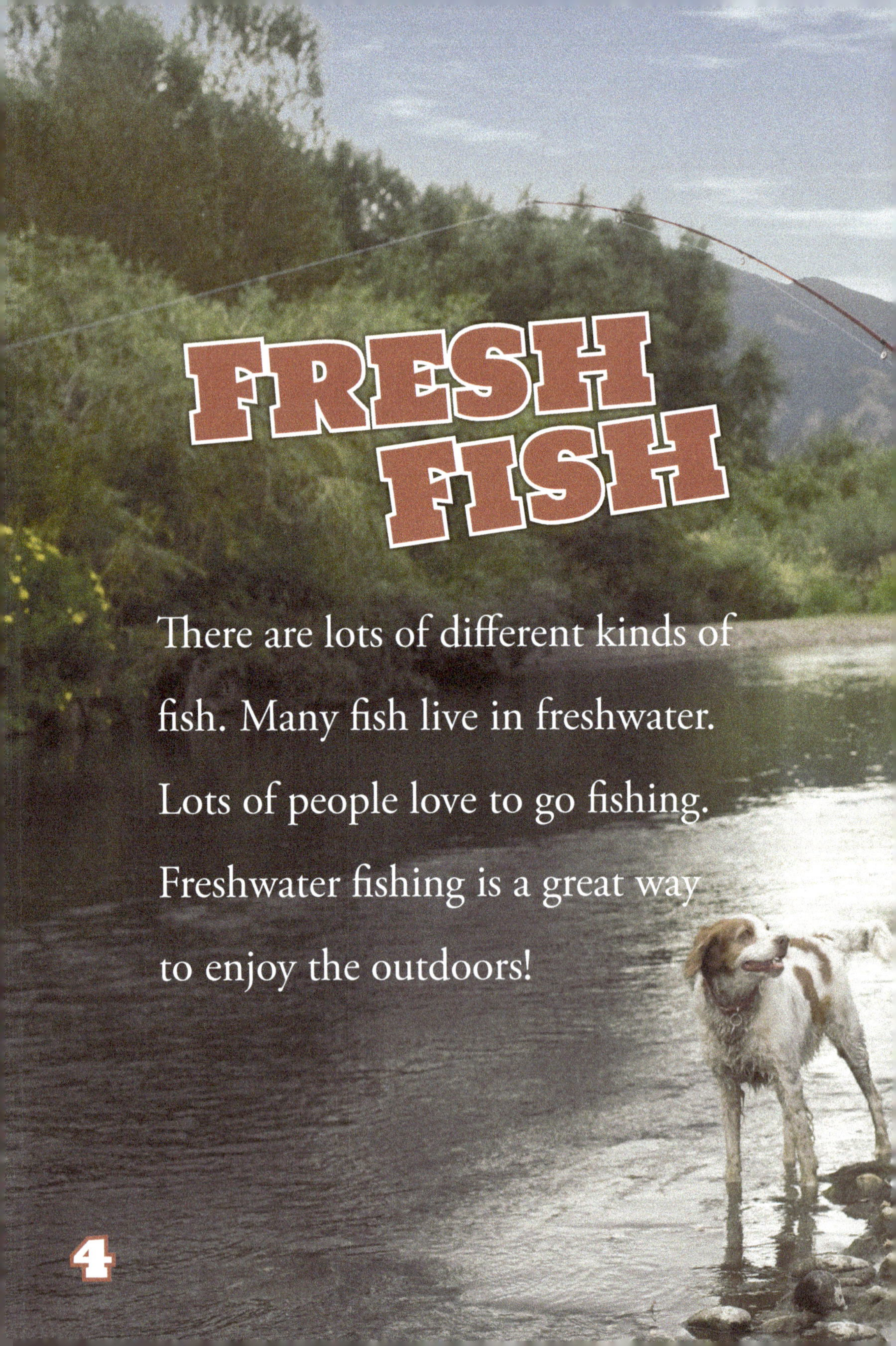

FRESH FISH

There are lots of different kinds of fish. Many fish live in freshwater. Lots of people love to go fishing. Freshwater fishing is a great way to enjoy the outdoors!

Freshwater fishing is any kind of fishing not done in the ocean. Lakes, ponds, rivers, and streams are all great places to go freshwater fishing.

Some people freshwater fish where freshwater mixes with salt water, like when a river meets an ocean. This is called a bay or **estuary**. The mixture of water is called **brackish** water.

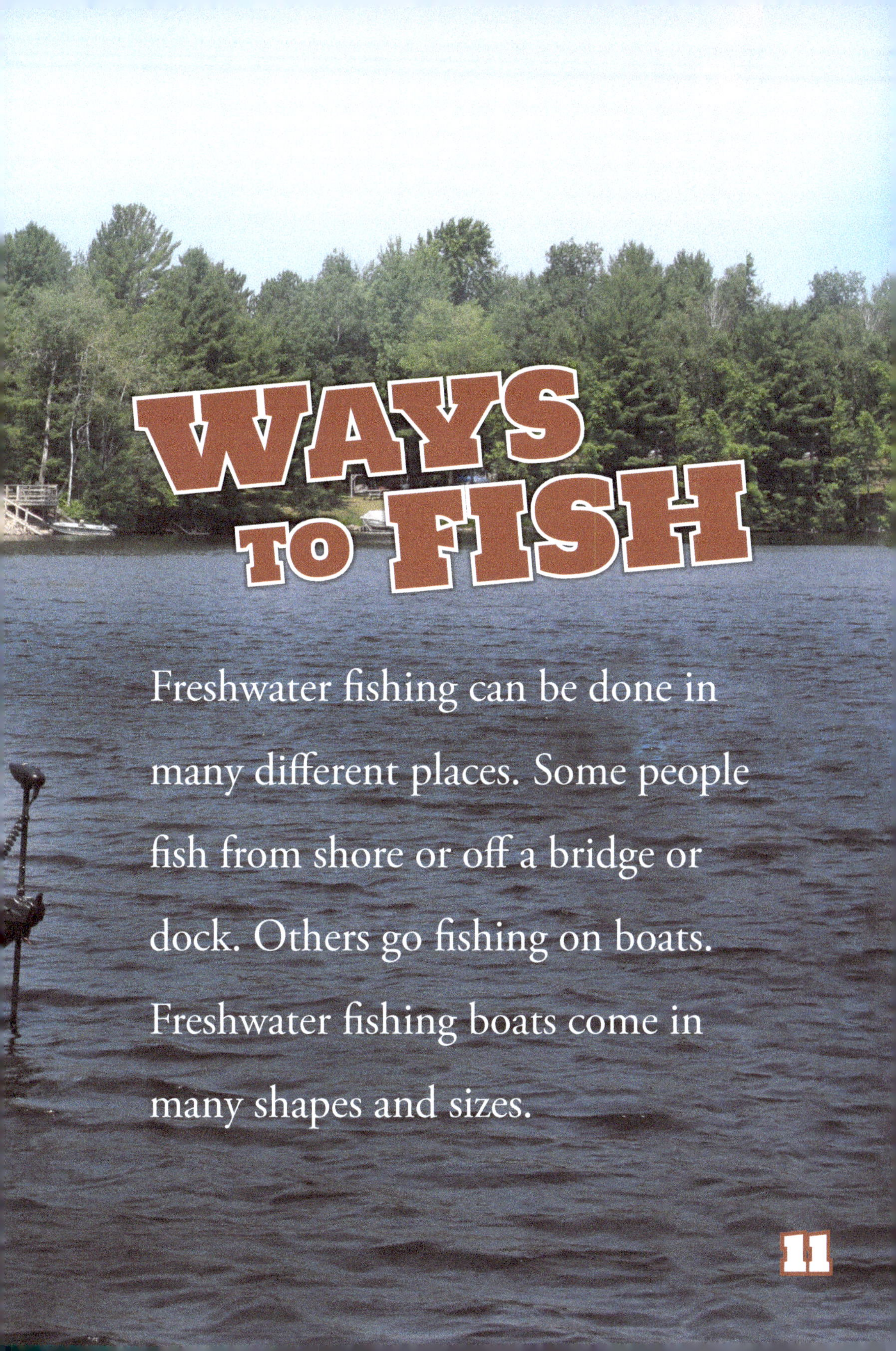

WAYS TO FISH

Freshwater fishing can be done in many different places. Some people fish from shore or off a bridge or dock. Others go fishing on boats. Freshwater fishing boats come in many shapes and sizes.

About 40 percent of all fish are freshwater fish. Fish such as salmon and catfish make for great freshwater fishing. Many freshwater fish, such as bass and trout, are found all over the world.

TOOL TIME

There are many things a fisherman needs to go freshwater fishing. Picking the right tools can make the difference between getting a big catch and coming away empty-handed!

Freshwater fishing rods are similar to most fishing poles. They're made of a pole and a fishing line. The long fishing line is connected to a **reel**, which winds up and collects the line.

RIGGING IT

Fishermen use different **knots** and rigs to catch different fish. A rig is the type of knot, **bait**, and hook you use to catch a fish. There are many different kinds of rigs to catch freshwater fish.

To freshwater fish, a fisherman casts the fishing pole into the water. A weight on the end of the rig helps the cast reach farther away from the pole. The weight sometimes stays on top of the water. This is called a bobber.

SET THE HOOK

The fisherman reels in the line and casts it back out until a fish takes the bait. Next, the fisherman needs to set the hook. They raise the fishing pole up very fast. This makes sure the fish doesn't get away.

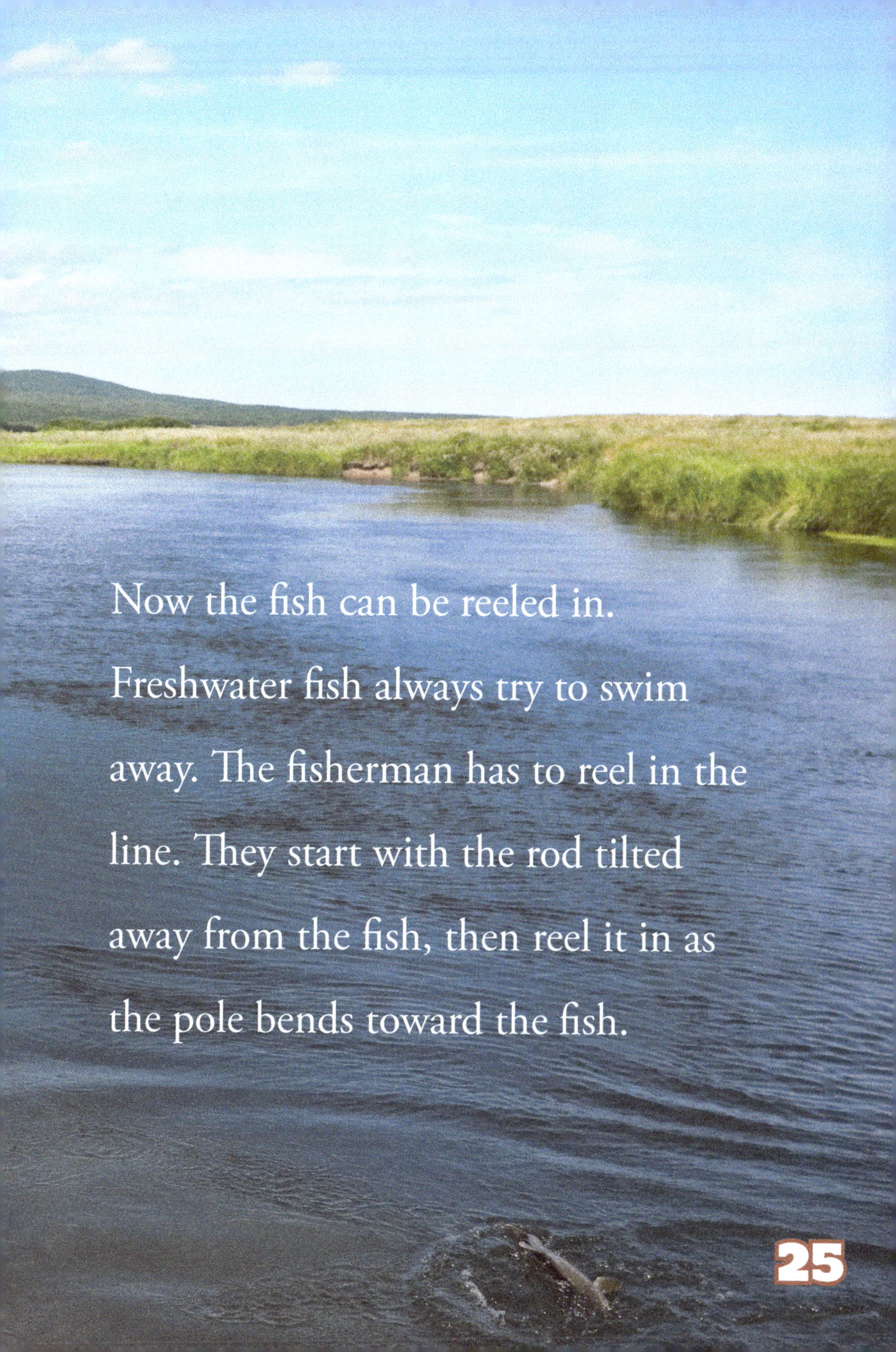

Now the fish can be reeled in. Freshwater fish always try to swim away. The fisherman has to reel in the line. They start with the rod tilted away from the fish, then reel it in as the pole bends toward the fish.

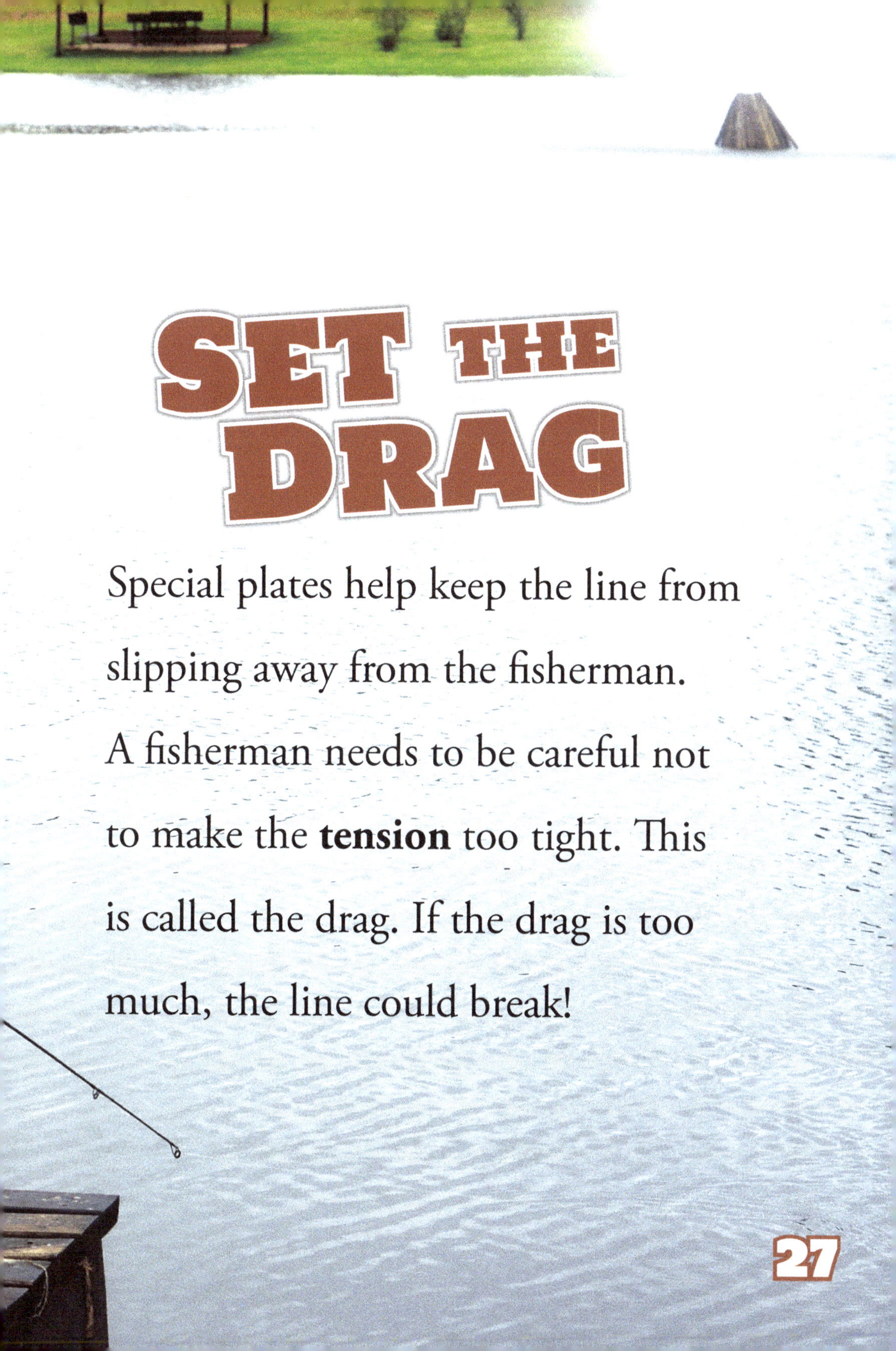

SET THE DRAG

Special plates help keep the line from slipping away from the fisherman. A fisherman needs to be careful not to make the **tension** too tight. This is called the drag. If the drag is too much, the line could break!

CATCH AND RELEASE

When the fish gets close to the fisherman, it pops out of the water. The fish gets caught with a net. Some people keep the fish to eat. Others throw the fish back into the water. This is called catch-and-release fishing.

FRESHWATER FISHING SAFETY

- Use the buddy system.
- Wear a life vest.
- Don't leave equipment on the ground.
- Be careful with hooks.
- Cast pole away from others.
- Don't cast toward other objects.

FOR MORE INFORMATION

Books

Green, Sara. *Freshwater Fishing*. Minneapolis, MN: Bellwether Media, 2013.

Lindeen, Carol. *Freshwater Fishing*. Mankato, MN: Capstone Press, 2011.

Schwartz, Tina P. *Freshwater Fishing*. New York, NY: PowerKids Press, 2012.

Websites

How to Land a Fish

takemefishing.org/fishing/fishopedia/how-to-fish/landing-the-fish
Learn how to get your catch in the boat or on land with these tips and videos.

What Is Freshwater Fishing?

takemefishing.org/fishing/freshwater-fishing/what-is-freshwater-fishing
Find tips and tricks about freshwater fishing on this great site.

GLOSSARY

bait: something used to attract another animal

brackish: being a mixture of freshwater and salt water

estuary: a place where an ocean tide meets a river current

knot: a tie of line or string that creates a lump

reel: a tool that is turned to gather fishing line, or to collect a fishing line

tension: to stretch something to create stiffness

INDEX